Wedding Planner ♡

Wedding Planner...

WEDDING DATE & TIME:

VENUE ADDRESS:

BUDGET:

OFFICIANT:

WEDDING PARTY:

TO DO LIST:

NOTES & REMINDERS:

Wedding Budget...

	TOTAL COST:	DEPOSIT:	REMAINDER:
WEDDING VENUE			
RECEPTION VENUE			
FLORIST			
OFFICIANT			
CATERER			
WEDDING CAKE			
BRIDAL ATTIRE			
GROOM ATTIRE			
BRIDAL JEWELRY			
BRIDESMAID ATTIRE			
GROOMSMEN ATTIRE			
HAIR & MAKE UP			
PHOTOGRAPHER			
VIDEOGRAPHER			
DJ SERVICE/ENTERTAINMENT			
INVITATIONS			
TRANSPORTATION			
WEDDING PARTY GIFTS			
RENTALS			
HONEYMOON			

12 Months Before...

- SET THE DATE
- SET YOUR BUDGET
- CHOOSE YOUR THEME
- ORGANIZE ENGAGEMENT PARTY
- RESEARCH VENUES
- BOOK A WEDDING PLANNER
- RESEARCH PHOTOGRAPHERS
- RESEARCH VIDEOGRAPHERS
- RESEARCH DJ'S/ENTERTAINMENT

- CONSIDER FLORISTS
- RESEARCH CATERERS
- DECIDE ON OFFICIANT
- CREATE INITIAL GUEST LIST
- CHOOSE WEDDING PARTY
- SHOP FOR WEDDING DRESS
- REGISTER WITH GIFT REGISTRY
- DISCUSS HONEYMOON IDEAS
- RESEARCH WEDDING RINGS

THINGS TO REMEMBER:

9 Months Before...

- FINALIZE GUEST LIST
- ORDER INVITATIONS
- PLAN YOUR RECEPTION
- BOOK PHOTOGRAPHER
- BOOK VIDEOGRAPHER
- BOOK FLORIST
- BOOK DJ/ENTERTAINMENT
- BOOK CATERER
- CHOOSE WEDDING CAKE

- CHOOSE WEDDING GOWN
- ORDER BRIDESMAIDS DRESSES
- RESERVE TUXEDOS
- ARRANGE TRANSPORTATION
- BOOK WEDDING VENUE
- BOOK RECEPTION VENUE
- PLAN HONEYMOON
- BOOK OFFICIANT
- BOOK ROOMS FOR GUESTS

THINGS TO REMEMBER:

6 Months Before...

- ORDER THANK YOU NOTES
- REVIEW RECEPTION DETAILS
- MAKE APPT FOR DRESS FITTING
- CONFIRM BRIDEMAIDS DRESSES
- GET MARRIAGE LICENSE

- BOOK HAIR/MAKE UP STYLIST
- CONFIRM MUSIC SELECTIONS
- PLAN BRIDAL SHOWER
- PLAN REHEARSAL
- SHOP FOR WEDDING RINGS

THINGS TO REMEMBER:

3 Months Before...

- MAIL OUT INVITATIONS
- MEET WITH OFFICIANT
- BUY GIFTS FOR WEDDING PARTY
- BOOK FINAL GOWN FITTING
- BUY WEDDING BANDS
- PLAN YOUR HAIR STYLE
- PURCHASE SHOES/HEELS
- CONFIRM PASSPORTS ARE VALID

- FINALIZE RECEPTION MENU
- PLAN REHEARSAL DINNER
- CONFIRM ALL BOOKINGS
- APPLY FOR MARRIAGE LICENSE
- CONFIRM MUSIC SELECTIONS
- DRAFT WEDDING VOWS
- CHOOSE YOUR MC
- ARRANGE AIRPORT TRANSFER

THINGS TO REMEMBER:

1 Month Before...

- CONFIRM FINAL GUEST COUNT
- CONFIRM RECEPTION DETAILS
- ATTEND FINAL GOWN FITTING
- CONFIRM PHOTOGRAPHER
- WRAP WEDDING PARTY GIFTS
- CREATE PHOTOGRAPHY SHOT LIST

- REHEARSE WEDDING VOWS
- BOOK MANI-PEDI
- CONFIRM WITH FLORIST
- CONFIRM VIDEOGRAPHER
- PICK UP BRIDEMAIDS DRESSES
- CREATE WEDDING SCHEDULE

THINGS TO REMEMBER:

1 Week Before...

- FINALIZE SEATING PLANS
- MAKE PAYMENTS TO VENDORS
- PACK FOR HONEYMOON
- CONFIRM HOTEL RESERVATIONS
- GIVE SCHEDULE TO PARTY
- DELIVER LICENSE TO OFFICIANT
- CONFIRM WITH BAKERY
- PICK UP WEDDING DRESS
- PICK UP TUXEDOS
- GIVE MUSIC LIST TO DJ

THINGS TO REMEMBER:

1 Week Before...

THINGS TO DO: NOTES:

MONDAY

TUESDAY

WEDNESDAY

THURSDAY

REMINDERS & NOTES:

1 Week Before...

	THINGS TO DO:	NOTES:
FRIDAY		
SATURDAY		
SUNDAY		

LEFT TO DO:

REMINDERS:

NOTES:

The Day Before...

- ☐ GET MANICURE/PEDICURE
- ☐ ATTEND REHEARSAL DINNER
- ☐ GET A GOOD NIGHT'S SLEEP!
- ☐ GIVE GIFTS TO WEDDING PARTY
- ☐ FINALIZE PACKING

TO DO LIST:

The Big Day!

- [ ] GET HAIR & MAKE UP DONE
- [ ] HAVE A HEALTHY BREAKFAST
- [ ] ENJOY YOUR BIG DAY!
- [ ] MEET WITH BRIDESMAIDS
- [ ] GIVE RINGS TO BEST MAN

TO DO LIST:

Wedding Planner...

ENGAGEMENT PARTY:

DATE: _____ LOCATION: _____

TIME: _____ NUMBER OF GUESTS: _____

NOTES:

BRIDAL SHOWER:

DATE: _____ LOCATION: _____

TIME: _____ NUMBER OF GUESTS: _____

NOTES:

STAG & DOE PARTY:

DATE: _____ LOCATION: _____

TIME: _____ NUMBER OF GUESTS: _____

NOTES:

Wedding Party

MAID/MATRON OF HONOR:

PHONE: _____ DRESS SIZE: _____ SHOE SIZE: _____

EMAIL: _____

BRIDESMAID:

PHONE: _____ DRESS SIZE: _____ SHOE SIZE: _____

EMAIL: _____

BRIDESMAID #2:

PHONE: _____ DRESS SIZE: _____ SHOE SIZE: _____

EMAIL: _____

BRIDESMAID #3:

PHONE: _____ DRESS SIZE: _____ SHOE SIZE: _____

EMAIL: _____

BRIDESMAID #4:

PHONE: _____ DRESS SIZE: _____ SHOE SIZE: _____

EMAIL: _____

Wedding Party

BEST MAN:

PHONE: WAIST SIZE: SHOE SIZE:

NECK SIZE: SLEEVE SIZE: JACKET SIZE:

EMAIL:

GROOMSMEN #1:

PHONE: WAIST SIZE: SHOE SIZE:

NECK SIZE: SLEEVE SIZE: JACKET SIZE:

EMAIL:

GROOMSMEN #2:

PHONE: WAIST SIZE: SHOE SIZE:

NECK SIZE: SLEEVE SIZE: JACKET SIZE:

EMAIL:

GROOMSMEN #3:

PHONE: WAIST SIZE: SHOE SIZE:

NECK SIZE: SLEEVE SIZE: JACKET SIZE:

EMAIL:

GROOMSMEN #4:

PHONE: WAIST SIZE: SHOE SIZE:

NECK SIZE: SLEEVE SIZE: JACKET SIZE:

EMAIL:

Photographer

PHOTOGRAPHER:

PHONE: _____ COMPANY: _____

EMAIL: _____ ADDRESS: _____

WEDDING PACKAGE OVERVIEW:

EST PRICE: _____

INCLUSIONS:	YES ✓	NO ✓	COST:
ENGAGEMENT SHOOT:	☐	☐	
PHOTO ALBUMS:	☐	☐	
FRAMES:	☐	☐	
PROOFS INCLUDED:	☐	☐	
NEGATIVES INCLUDED:	☐	☐	

TOTAL COST:

Videographer

VIDEOGRAPHER:

PHONE: _____   COMPANY: _____

EMAIL: _____   ADDRESS: _____

WEDDING PACKAGE OVERVIEW:

EST PRICE: _____

INCLUSIONS:	YES ✓	NO ✓	COST:
DUPLICATES/COPIES:			
PHOTO MONTAGE:			
MUSIC ADDED:			
EDITING:			

TOTAL COST: _____

DJ/Entertainment

DJ/LIVE BAND/ENTERTAINMENT:

PHONE: COMPANY:

EMAIL: ADDRESS:

START TIME: END TIME:

ENTERTAINMENT SERVICE OVERVIEW:

EST PRICE:

INCLUSIONS:	YES ✓	NO ✓	COST:
SOUND EQUIPMENT:	☐	☐	
LIGHTING:	☐	☐	
SPECIAL EFFECTS:	☐	☐	
GRATUITIES	☐	☐	

TOTAL COST:

Florist Planner

FLORIST:

PHONE: _____ COMPANY: _____

EMAIL: _____ ADDRESS: _____

FLORAL PACKAGE:

EST PRICE: _____

INCLUSIONS:	YES ✓	NO ✓	COST:
BRIDAL BOUQUET:	☐	☐	
THROW AWAY BOUQUET:	☐	☐	
CORSAGES:	☐	☐	
CEREMONY FLOWERS	☐	☐	
CENTERPIECES	☐	☐	
CAKE TOPPER	☐	☐	
BOUTONNIERE	☐	☐	

TOTAL COST:

Wedding Cake

PHONE: COMPANY:

EMAIL: ADDRESS:

WEDDING CAKE PACKAGE:

COST: _____ FREE TASTING: _____ DELIVERY FEE: _____

FLAVOR:

FILLING:

SIZE:

SHAPE:

COLOR:

EXTRAS:

TOTAL COST:

Transportation Planner

TO CEREMONY: PICK UP TIME: PICK UP LOCATION:

BRIDE:

GROOM:

BRIDE'S PARENTS:

GROOM'S PARENTS:

BRIDESMAIDS:

GROOMSMEN:

NOTES:

TO RECEPTION: PICK UP TIME: PICK UP LOCATION:

BRIDE & GROOM:

BRIDE'S PARENTS:

GROOM'S PARENTS:

BRIDESMAIDS:

GROOMSMEN:

Wedding Planner...

BACHELORETTE PARTY:

DATE: _____   LOCATION: _____

TIME: _____   NUMBER OF GUESTS: _____

NOTES:

BACHELOR PARTY:

DATE: _____   LOCATION: _____

TIME: _____   NUMBER OF GUESTS: _____

NOTES:

CEREMONY REHEARSAL:

DATE: _____   LOCATION: _____

TIME: _____   NUMBER OF GUESTS: _____

NOTES:

Wedding Planner...

REHEARSAL DINNER:

DATE: _____ LOCATION: _____

TIME: _____ NUMBER OF GUESTS: _____

NOTES:

RECEPTION:

DATE: _____ LOCATION: _____

TIME: _____ NUMBER OF GUESTS: _____

NOTES:

REMINDERS:

Names & Addresses

CEREMONY:

PHONE: CONTACT NAME:

EMAIL: ADDRESS:

RECEPTION:

PHONE: CONTACT NAME:

EMAIL: ADDRESS:

OFFICIANT:

PHONE: CONTACT NAME:

EMAIL: ADDRESS:

WEDDING PLANNER:

PHONE: CONTACT NAME:

EMAIL: ADDRESS:

Names & Addresses

CATERER:

PHONE: CONTACT NAME:

EMAIL: ADDRESS:

FLORIST:

PHONE: CONTACT NAME:

EMAIL: ADDRESS:

BAKERY:

PHONE: CONTACT NAME:

EMAIL: ADDRESS:

BRIDAL SHOP:

PHONE: CONTACT NAME:

EMAIL: ADDRESS:

Names & Addresses

PHOTOGRAPHER:

PHONE: CONTACT NAME:

EMAIL: ADDRESS:

VIDEOGRAPHER:

PHONE: CONTACT NAME:

EMAIL: ADDRESS:

DJ/ENTERTAINMENT:

PHONE: CONTACT NAME:

EMAIL: ADDRESS:

HAIR/NAIL SALON:

PHONE: CONTACT NAME:

EMAIL: ADDRESS:

Names & Addresses

MAKE UP ARTIST:

PHONE: _____   CONTACT NAME: _____

EMAIL: _____   ADDRESS: _____

RENTALS:

PHONE: _____   CONTACT NAME: _____

EMAIL: _____   ADDRESS: _____

HONEYMOON RESORT/HOTEL:

PHONE: _____   CONTACT NAME: _____

EMAIL: _____   ADDRESS: _____

TRANSPORTATION SERVICE:

PHONE: _____   CONTACT NAME: _____

EMAIL: _____   ADDRESS: _____

Caterer Details

CONTACT INFORMATION:

PHONE: _____   CONTACT NAME: _____

EMAIL: _____   ADDRESS: _____

MENU CHOICE #1:

MENU CHOICE #2:

	YES ✓	NO ✓	COST:
BAR INCLUDED:	☐	☐	
CORKAGE FEE:	☐	☐	
HORS D'OEURS:	☐	☐	
TAXES INCLUDED:	☐	☐	
GRATUITIES INCLUDED:	☐	☐	

HORS D'OEUVRES

1st COURSE:

2nd COURSE:

3rd COURSE:

4th COURSE:

DESSERT:

Menu Planner

COFFEE/TEA:

FRUIT:

SWEETS TABLE:

WEDDING CAKE:

NOTES:

Wedding Guest List

NAME:	ADDRESS:	# IN PARTY:	RSVP ✓
Ronald Podlaski			
James Podlaski			
Jacqueline Brown			
Liza Brown			
Doug Smith			
Elloin			
Mike			
Geraldine Podlaski			
Romello Lindsey			
Geonna Wilson			
Saphrina Denney			
Molly Osowski			
Corey Baker			
Andrew			
JR			
Shayla			
Mike			
Bud Murphy			
Barbara Murphy			
Jessie Amato			

Wedding Guest List

NAME:	ADDRESS:	# IN PARTY:	RSVP✓
Jesse Murphy			
Heidi Murphy			
Anita Podlaski			
Richard Podlaski			
Martha			
Julie Rolf			
Ted Rolf			
Simon Rolf			
Theo Rolf			
Albi Rolf			
Trainer Rolf			
Scott Smith			
Woody Smith			
Lauren Smith			
Mikey			
Joan			
Blind Man Drew			
Nash			
Bash			
Stash			

Wedding Guest List

NAME:	ADDRESS:	# IN PARTY:	RSVP ✓
Yeti			
Zach McManus			
Geno			
Sally			
Jack Arpert			
Noa			
Jake White			
Stella			
Caroline O'connor			
Corey O'connor			
O'connor Parents		2	

Wedding Guest List

NAME:	ADDRESS:	# IN PARTY:	RSVP✓

Wedding Guest List

NAME:	ADDRESS:	# IN PARTY:	RSVP✓

Wedding Guest List

NAME:	ADDRESS:	# IN PARTY:	RSVP✓

Wedding Guest List

NAME:	ADDRESS:	# IN PARTY:	RSVP ✓

Wedding Guest List

NAME:	ADDRESS:	# IN PARTY:	RSVP✓

Wedding Guest List

NAME:	ADDRESS:	# IN PARTY:	RSVP✓

Wedding Guest List

NAME:	ADDRESS:	# IN PARTY:	RSVP✓

Wedding Guest List

NAME:	ADDRESS:	# IN PARTY:	RSVP ✓

Wedding Guest List

NAME:	ADDRESS:	# IN PARTY:	RSVP ✓

Wedding Guest List

NAME:	ADDRESS:	# IN PARTY:	RSVP ✓

Wedding Guest List

NAME:	ADDRESS:	# IN PARTY:	RSVP✓

Wedding Guest List

NAME:	ADDRESS:	# IN PARTY:	RSVP✓

Wedding Guest List

NAME:	ADDRESS:	# IN PARTY:	RSVP ✓

Wedding Guest List

NAME:	ADDRESS:	# IN PARTY:	RSVP ✓

Wedding Guest List

NAME:	ADDRESS:	# IN PARTY:	RSVP✓

Wedding Guest List

NAME:	ADDRESS:	# IN PARTY:	RSVP✓

Wedding Guest List

NAME:	ADDRESS:	# IN PARTY:	RSVP✓

Seating Planner

Table #

Table #

Seating Planner

Table #

Table #

Seating Planner

Table #

Table #

Seating Planner

Table #

Table #

Seating Planner

Table #

Table #

Seating Planner

Table #

Table #

Seating Planner

Table #

Table #

Seating Planner

Table #

Table #

Seating Planner

Table #

Table #

Seating Planner

Table #

Table #

Seating Planner

Table #

Table #

Seating Planner

Table #

Table #

Seating Planner

Table #

Table #

Seating Planner

Table #

Table #

Seating Planner

Table #

Table #

Seating Planner

Table #

Table #

Seating Planner

Table #

Table #

Seating Planner

Table #

Table #

Seating Planner

Table #

Table #

Seating Planner

Table #

Table #

Seating Planner

Table #

Table #

Seating Planner

Table #

Table #

Seating Planner

Table #

Table #

Seating Planner

Table #

Table #

Seating Planner

Table #

Table #

Seating Planner

Table #

Table #

Location Ideas:

New England:

1. Ocean
2. Bud + Barbara's Yard
3. Molly's Grandparents house
4. Tree House Burlington Park
5. Rockingham Farm (Flannel Fest Place)

Colorado:

1. Trout Lake
2. Aldisaro?
3. Moab BLM
4. Gateway BLM

Honeymoon Ideas:
① Cambodia + Thailand ★
② Whistler
③ Iceland
④ Greece/Turkey
⑤ Bali
⑥ Maldives/Bora-Bora
⑦ Italy
⑧ Norway
⑨ New Zealand
⑩ Japan

Every 5 years we will celebrate our milestone anniversary by choosing another place we wanted to go to ♡

Made in the USA
Middletown, DE
16 May 2021